RoBots Rule!

Written by Sandy Fussell

Illustrated by Nathan Jurevicius

Park Academy
Robin Hoods Wall
Boston
PE21 9LQ

Published by Pearson Education Limited, 80 Strand, London, WC2R 0RL.

www.pearsonschools.co.uk

First published in 2010 by Pearson Australia.
This edition of *Robots Rule!* is published by Pearson Education Limited
by arrangement with Pearson Australia. All rights reserved.

Text © Pearson Australia 2010
Text by Sandy Fussell

Original illustrations © Pearson Australia 2010
Illustrated by Nathan Jurevicius

22 21 20 19 18
10 9 8 7 6 5 4 3 2 1

British Library Cataloguing in Publication Data
A catalogue record for this book is available from the British Library

ISBN 978 0 435 19457 4

Copyright notice
All rights reserved. No part of this publication may be reproduced in any form or by any means (including photocopying or storing it in any medium by electronic means and whether or not transiently or incidentally to some other use of this publication) without the written permission of the copyright owner, except in accordance with the provisions of the Copyright, Designs and Patents Act 1988 or under the terms of a licence issued by the Copyright Licensing Agency, Barnards Inn, 86 Fetter Lane, London EC4A 1EN (www.cla.co.uk). Applications for the copyright owner's written permission should be addressed to the publisher.

Printed in China by Golden Cup

Acknowledgements
We would like to thank the following schools for their invaluable help in the development and trialling of the Bug Club resources: Bishop Road Primary School, Bristol; Blackhorse Primary School, Bristol; Hollingwood Primary School, West Yorkshire; Kingswood Parks Primary, Hull; Langdale CE Primary School, Ambleside; Pickering Infant School, Pickering; The Royal School, Wolverhampton; St Thomas More's Catholic Primary School, Hampshire; West Park Primary School, Wolverhampton.

Note from the publisher
Pearson has robust editorial processes, including answer and fact checks, to ensure the accuracy of the content in this publication, and every effort is made to ensure this publication is free of errors. We are, however, only human, and occasionally errors do occur. Pearson is not liable for any misunderstandings that arise as a result of errors in this publication, but it is our priority to ensure that the content is accurate. If you spot an error, please do contact us at resourcescorrections@pearson.com so we can make sure it is corrected.

Contents

Chapter One	Robot	5
Chapter Two	Skatebot	12
Chapter Three	BMXbot	21
Chapter Four	Surfbot	33
Chapter Five	Xbot	44

Chapter One
RoBot

It's just not fair. Everyone in my class is doing a really hard test this morning – except Jenna! Just because her parents are rich, Jenna's got her own robot to help her with her school work.

Miss Lin, our teacher, says there's nothing stopping me bringing in a robot to help me too – but my mum and dad can't afford expensive things like robots.

"Anyway," I think to myself, "if I had a robot I wouldn't bring it to school and use it to help me with my maths tests. If I had a robot, I'd take it to the skate park and teach it all the tricks I know."

"That sounds fun!" says a voice in my head.

I look around the classroom but everyone is writing on their test papers. Just then, I spot Jenna's robot winking at me. It must have been the robot's voice I heard in my head!

"I'd much rather be skateboarding," the voice says.

"Wow," I think. "I didn't know robots could transmit their thoughts!"

"Of course we can!" says the robot's voice in my head.

"Is something wrong, Rhianna?" Miss Lin is staring at me.

RoBot

I shake my head and pretend to be working on my test, but really, I'm listening to the robot.

"I want to go skateboarding," the robot transmits to me. "But I belong to Jenna, and she doesn't skate. In fact, she doesn't do anything interesting. She just plays hairdressers and dressing up, and something even worse."

"What could be worse than that?" I think-say back to the robot.

"Playing with dolls," the robot transmits.

It *is* worse. I feel sorry for the robot.

RoBots Rule!

"Okay, I'll take you skateboarding," I reply, "but you have to come up with a plan so that Jenna doesn't know."

The robot has the smartest brain in our class. I know it will be able to think of something.

It already has.

"Every morning Jenna leaves me at the back door while she feeds the neighbour's cat. You could collect me from there," it says.

"Wouldn't that be stealing?" I ask.

"No," the robot transmits firmly. "You would be rescuing me."

I have to save the robot from Jenna and her dolls.

"I'll do it," I decide.

"Can you bring me something to wear?" asks the robot. "Nothing in Jenna's wardrobe is suitable for skateboarding."

It won't be hard to disguise the robot. It's made of a special metal that looks like skin. You can't tell the difference except sometimes it shines in the sun. Most grown-ups can hardly tell the difference between robots and human children.

"Don't worry. I'll find something. What's your name?"

"It's silly," the robot says.

"I won't laugh. I promise."

RoBots Rule!

"Lucy Lee," the robot whispers.

"I can fix that." This time I wink. "Tomorrow you will be a SkateBot. That can be your new name."

Miss Lin is staring at me again. This time she looks angry. "Rhianna, you have hardly started your test."

"Sorry, Miss Lin."

"Are you sure about the answer to question one?" SkateBot asks me. I look at my test paper and realise I have made a mistake.

I check the rest of my answers quickly. I think I've got them all right. I add my name and the date at the top of the page. Rhianna Rix. 15 April, 2110.

Robots rule all right. I'm going to get full marks in a test and tomorrow it's the weekend. I'm going to go skateboarding with SkateBot!

Chapter Two
SkateBot

The morning sunshine pours into my bedroom window. It's a perfect day for skateboarding.

"Mum," I say. "May I go down to the skate park, please?"

"Well, okay," she says. "As long as you go with Jack."

SkateBot

Jack's my older brother. He can be a pain sometimes, but he's usually too busy doing his own things to stop me doing what I want to.

"No problem!" I say. "Jack's already down at the skate park – I'll see him there."

"All right," says Mum. "I'll ring Jack and check he knows to look out for you."

RoBots Rule!

Mum gives me some cash. "Here's some money so you can get yourself and Jack some lunch from the shop. Try to find something healthy."

"Thanks, Mum. Bye."
I race out of the front door before she can ask more questions.

I grab my skateboard from the garage. My board has super-fast wheels. The deck is the new carbon type. It took me seven months to save up for it, but it's a great board, the best in the whole school.

I skate down the street, practising my heel flips and a few other cool moves. I'm good at skating because I practise a lot.

Jenna lives in the next street, in a huge house with a shiny car in the driveway. But Jenna's not a spoilt, rich kid. She's really nice. I'm beginning to feel a bit guilty now.

I sneak up the side path. SkateBot is sitting at Jenna's back door.

RoBots Rule!

"Hello," it says. "Did you bring me some clothes?" The robot sounds like a real kid when it talks aloud.

I hand over a pair of skate shorts, a cap and my least favourite surf shirt. SkateBot dresses quickly.

"I brought a skateboard." SkateBot waves a board at me.

"Where did you get that?"

"It was in Jenna's garage," SkateBot says.

Jenna and her little brother are lucky. They have all the latest high-tech stuff.

The skate park isn't far away so it doesn't take long to skate there. I'm really fast and SkateBot is a quick learner.

"Hey," I say. "You're not doing badly for a beginner!"

"Thanks!" says SkateBot turning to look at me. "I don't mind if I'm not a fantastic skater. I just want to have fun."

SkateBot flips its skateboard and falls off.

Clunk.

Now there's a scratch on its arm.

"You can't do tricks properly if you don't look where you're going," I say.

SkateBot zooms ahead. I have to race to keep up.

The park has three ramps, a set of rails and a really cool half pipe. Jack and a couple of his friends are already in the park.

RoBots Rule!

"I think we might have a problem," I mutter.

"Why?"

"My brother's friends don't want little kids hanging around when they're practising."

"It's not their park. Robots' rule number one: age doesn't make you good at something."

SkateBot does a kick turn onto the front ramp.

SkateBot

I agree. I'm probably better than both Jack's friends – especially the one wearing the black shirt, Tom. He just fell off halfway up the pipe curve.

"Hey, you kids," Tom yells. "Clear off!"

"Why should we?" SkateBot yells back at him.

"This is our pipe," Tom says.

SkateBot pretends to read the graffiti on the pipe wall. "Is your name on it somewhere here?" it asks.

RoBots Rule!

"Don't be a smart alec," says Jack.

"He's new to skating. He doesn't mean it," I say.

SkateBot skids into the pipe and does a few tricks, looking quite cool.

"That's not bad." Tom whistles. "Let's see what you can do," he says to me.

I zoom into the pipe and do a high heel flip. I can tell Jack and his friends are impressed, though they don't say much.

"Okay," says Jack's other friend, Nate. "You two can stay this time. Don't get in our way."

SkateBot wants to argue but I shake my head to say no. It's a fair deal.

Chapter Three

BMXBot

From the top lip of the pipe, I can see the flags of a fair. Carnival music fills my ears and I can smell chips. Nothing beats a cone of hot chips, smothered in tomato sauce.

"Hey, SkateBot. Come up here," I call.

SkateBot charges up the ramp. Its shiny feet are covered in scratches.

"Look." I point towards the tents and sideshows. "Let's go and have some fun."

RoBots Rule!

I know Mum wouldn't want us to go off to the fair on our own, but luckily Jack's friends have to go home now. Jack agrees to come to the fair with us.

"Race you to the gate!" says SkateBot, whizzing across the grass.

"We need some more money," I say when I catch up. We only have the cash Mum gave me earlier. If I buy chips and a drink, there will be hardly any money left.

"Maybe we can win some money." says SkateBot, pointing to a stall where you knock over a stack of three cans to win. The top can has a five pound note taped to it.

I'm not sure this plan will work. Jack says most of the cans are filled with sand so it's really hard to knock all three over. "A few cans are empty to trick people into thinking they can do it," he goes on.

"Try your luck, kids. Easy money," the man on the stall yells.

SkateBot is already there.

"Have a try, kid," the man says. Like most grown-ups, he thinks SkateBot is human. "I'll give you three balls for nothing."

"Do we still get the money if we win?" I ask.

RoBots Rule!

"Of course you do!" The man grins. Most of his teeth are missing.

SkateBot throws the first ball. The can falls over.

Chunk.

"Your luck's in. Try again." The man doesn't seem surprised. Maybe that was the empty can.

SkateBot knocks over the other two. The man isn't so friendly now, and he doesn't seem keen to give us the money.

"It was the wind knocking the cans down," says the man. "Try again."

"No," says Jack.

"Yes," SkateBot says.

SkateBot knocks all the cans over.

Chunk, chunk, clunk.

"There's something funny about you," the man says, staring at SkateBot.

BMXBot

RoBots Rule!

"We'll have our money now." I pretend to be brave but my legs are shaking.

The man hands over the money. He's still staring at SkateBot.

"Let's go." I drag SkateBot into a run.

"Come back here," the man shouts.

SkateBot, Jack and I run and hide behind a van selling food.

"You showed that cheat." I slap SkateBot on the back.

Kerplunk.

When SkateBot laughs it sounds like the clatter of saucepan lids.

I buy cones of chips and two drinks, for me and Jack. SkateBot doesn't eat food, so it'll never know how good chips taste. I'm almost finished when SkateBot grabs my arm. I spill half my drink.

"Look." It points to the far edge of the fairground.

"What is it?" I can't see that far without robot vision.

"A BMX track."

RoBots Rule!

Jack doesn't want to go, so we agree to meet up later. I race off after SkateBot. By the time I catch up, it's already there, talking to the man in charge of the BMX track.

"Come on," says SkateBot. "Let's go!"

I look in my pocket. I wish I hadn't bought all those chips.

"Sorry, SkateBot," I say. "We haven't enough money."

I look at the man,
but he shakes his head.

"Sorry," he says.
"No money, no ride."

Then I hear a
familiar voice and my
stomach churns.

"Thieving kids. I've found you now. Give me back my money!" It's the man from the tin can stall.

"Calm down. What's wrong, Bill?" says the BMX man.

"These kids ripped me off."

"You mean these kids knocked over those cans full of sand and won some money from you?" The BMX man starts laughing.

Bill looks furious and stomps off, muttering under his breath.

"In you go, kids." The BMX man opens the gate. "You deserve a free ride after all. I'll mind your skateboards."

RoBots Rule!

BMXBot

We grab bikes and helmets. We ride across the bridge and zoom down the ramp. SkateBot is now BMXBot. We do wheelies on the track and fall off lots of times. BMXBot puts a huge dent in its leg.

"We're awful at this," I say, picking myself up off the ground.

"Robots' rule number two: you don't have to be good at something to have fun."

BMXBot tries a handlebar twist and falls in a heap. **Clank!**

Now there's a dent in its back, too.

RoBots Rule!

We ride until the BMX man blows a whistle to tell us our turn has ended.

"I'll take you back to Jenna's house," I say.

"No," says BMXBot.

"Why not?"

"I'm not going home, I'm coming with you. Tomorrow I want to go surfing."

BMXBot isn't thinking straight. Maybe falling off the bike has scrambled its brain. How could a robot go surfing? Robots are made of metal and metal rusts in salt water.

"Let's see what the weather is like tomorrow," I say. Maybe it will rain.

Chapter Four
SurfBot

When we catch up with Jack, I borrow his phone to ring Mum. I ask if my friend can stay for a sleepover. I'm sure she won't notice that BMXBot is a robot.

"I like your T-shirt," Mum says to BMXBot, when we get home. "Rhianna has one just like it but she won't wear it. She says it's not cool."

RoBots Rule!

"This is my favourite shirt," says BMXBot. Mum now likes the robot best of all my friends. She doesn't know it only has one T-shirt and that T-shirt belongs to me.

I show BMXBot my bedroom. It spends a lot of time looking at my posters – skateboarding, BMX bike riding and surfing. All extreme sports. BMXBot plants its foot and pretends to ride a wave.

"How can you surf?" I ask. "You're made of tin."

"No, I'm made of cast iron metal alloy. I'm rustproof." BMXBot laughs with a 'clank, clank' sound.

Mum says as a special treat we can have pizza for dinner. It's easy to eat lots of pizza so Mum thinks BMXBot ate some, too.

Next morning, the sun is shining. It's a beautiful day for surfing so I tell Mum we would like to go for a surf.

"You can't go on your own. I'm sure Jack will be going down to the beach if the surf is good. Ask him to take you," she says.

RoBots Rule!

Going with my elder brother is better than not going at all.

"I see you're wearing the same shirt," Mum says to BMXBot.

"It's my favourite."

"I've got a spare set of surfing gear," I say, handing BMXBot a bag. I call out to Jack to see if he is going for a surf.

"Yeah." A muffled reply comes from his bedroom.

"Can you take me and my friend?" I ask. "Mum said to ask you."

He groans. "Okay. I'll be ready to go in about twenty minutes."

I grab my boogie board. I find Jack's old boogie board for BMXBot. Jack doesn't use it now that he has got a surfboard. Now BMXBot is SurfBot.

"Some people think boogie boards are for losers. They say it's not really surfing," I say.

"Robots' rule number three: you don't need all the right gear to be part of something," says SurfBot

"Where do you get all this stuff about rules?" I ask.

"I find it in my brain."

I wish I could do that.

It doesn't take long to walk to the beach. When we get there, we can't wait to get into the sea and start surfing. Jack tells us to stay between the flags where the lifesavers are watching. He waves and heads out into the surf with his mates.

RoBots Rule!

SurfBot

SurfBot and I sit on the sand watching the waves crash against the shore. SurfBot is afraid. The ocean is scary when you've never been in it before.

"Come on," I say, pulling it up by its dented arm. "Let's do this together."

I teach SurfBot how to boogie board.

Soon, SurfBot is feeling happy in the water. It's having fun on the boogie board.

After lunch, two mums and their toddlers arrive at the beach. They set up an umbrella, and unpack towels and toys. SurfBot recognises one of the kids. He lives next door to Jenna.

All of a sudden, I'm worried about SurfBot being recognised. What if the toddler spots him and says something? Little kids notice everything. We might get caught. Time to go!

RoBots Rule!

"Let's go that way." I point to the rocks at the southern end of the beach. "We can go for a walk. Sometimes, there are interesting things in the rock pools."

In one of the rock pools, SurfBot finds a small jellyfish.

"I hope it's not a poisonous one!" I say. I don't want to touch it.

"I could give it a poke," says SurfBot. "Then we'll see if it tries to sting me."

"No!" I say. "Some jellyfish are really poisonous! Be careful!" I pull SurfBot away.

SurfBot looks sad. "It doesn't matter to me," it says. "The poison won't hurt me. I'm empty inside."

"No, you're not," I say. "You have a wonderful brain and you're a lot of fun to be with."

"No, I'm just circuits and switches."

Clink, clink. SurfBot tries to laugh but it sounds more like crying.

"Listen to me," I say. "That's rubbish. You've forgotten the robot rules. Age doesn't make you good at something, you don't even have to be good at something to have fun and you don't need the right gear to join in. You need a heart to know stuff like that," I say. "Kids' rule number one: whether you're human or a robot, you can still be a good friend."

It's the smartest thing I've ever said.

"Thanks." SurfBot gives me a friendly punch in the arm. **Clank.** I punch SurfBot back, carefully. I don't want to make another dent.

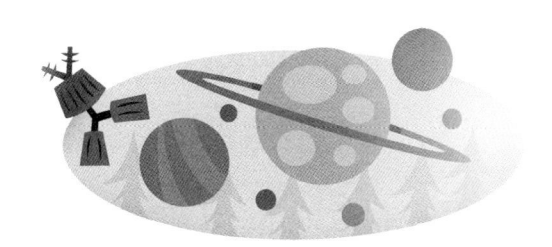

RoBots Rule!

"Race you." SurfBot is running. Its shiny legs are pounding up the beach.

"Where to?" I call, struggling to keep up.

"Home. It's time for me to go home to Jenna."

I let Jack know we're leaving and give him a wave.

"Do you have to go?" I ask SurfBot.

"Yes. The weekend is almost over and Jenna needs me for school."

SurfBot is right. All good things must come to an end. I bet Miss Lin has a really hard test waiting for me tomorrow. But what am I going to say to Jenna?

Chapter Five
XBot

"I see your robot is here again today, Jenna," says Miss Lin. "I hope it isn't giving you too much help?"

"No, Miss Lin. It says I should do the tests on my own."

"Good girl. All my students are smarter than they think they are and none of them needs a robot to help them." Miss Lin looks at me.

I start writing on my test paper. Secretly I hope SurfBot will give me the answers but nothing new appears in my brain. I glance over at the robot. Its eyes are closed. The test isn't hard after all and I manage to finish it all on my own. Jenna finishes almost as quickly as me.

At break time, I try to avoid her but she tracks me down. You can't hide from Jenna when she's on the warpath.

"I know what you did," she says.

RoBots Rule!

I think about the scrape on SurfBot's back, the scratches on its feet and the dents in its arms, legs and back.

"I'm sorry," I say.

"You should be. My robot told me everything."

"Oh," I say.

"You stole it and you returned it all dented. You owe me big time."

Fair enough. I nod in guilty agreement.

"Sorry," I say again.

Jenna crosses her arms and starts to tell me my punishment. "From now on you are responsible for taking my robot skateboarding, BMX biking and surfing."

I am amazed! My mouth is wide open and I am staring at Jenna. She giggles.

"Well, I don't like doing things like that," she says. "Now that my robot is an ExtremeBot, someone has to do those crazy things with it."

"You're not angry?" I can't believe it.

"I was at first," said Jenna. "But then my robot explained it all to me. It said it was partly my fault because I never listened to it." Jenna shook her head. "Anyway, now I do listen, and we talk a lot."

"I'm glad," I say.

"Really, I should thank you," says Jenna. "It's because of you that I've discovered I can be friends with XBot."

"XBot?" I ask.

RoBots Rule!

"A skateboarding, BMX-riding, surfing robot needs a special name. An eXtreme name – XBot."

Then she smiles. She might not like the same things as I do, but Jenna is all right.